MW00569527

ESSENTIAL CONCEPTS IN COMPUTER SCIENCE

ALGORITHMS

THE BUILDING BLOCKS OF COMPUTER PROGRAMMING

DANIEL R. FAUST

PowerKiDS press.

New York

Published in 2019 by The Rosen Publishing Group, Inc.
29 East 21st Street, New York, NY 10010

Copyright © 2019 by The Rosen Publishing Group, Inc.

All rights reserved. No part of this book may be reproduced in any form without permission in writing from the publisher, except by a reviewer.

First Edition

Editor: Jane Katirgis
Book Design: Reann Nye

Photo Credits: Cover Umberto Shtanzman/Shutterstock.com; p. 5 JGI/Tom Grill/Blend Images/Getty Images; p. 6 SVF2/Universal Images Group/Getty Images; p. 7 Compassionate Eye Foundation/Steven Errico/DigitalVision/Getty Images; pp. 9, 24 wavebreakmedia/Shutterstock.com; p. 11 Arina P Habich/Shutterstock.com; p. 13 Eternity in an Instant/DigitalVision/Getty Images; p. 15 Vintage Tone/Shutterstock.com; p. 17 Sergey Nivens/Shutterstock.com; p. 19 veeterzy/Shutterstock.com; p. 21 Arjuna Kodisinghe/Shutterstock.com; p. 23 Hero Images/Getty Images; p. 25 DEA/S. VANNINI/De Agostini/Getty Images; p. 27 Rawpixel.com/Shutterstock.com; p. 28 Denys Prykhodov/Shutterstock.com; p. 29 Corepics VOF/Shutterstock.com; p. 30 JGI/Tom Grill/Blend Images/Getty Images.

Cataloging-in-Publication Data

Names: Faust, Daniel R.
Title: Algorithms: the building blocks of computer programming / Daniel R. Faust.
Description: New York : PowerKids Press, 2019. | Series: Essential concepts in computer science | Includes glossary and index.
Identifiers: LCCN ISBN 9781538331286 (pbk.) | ISBN 9781538331279 (library bound) | ISBN 9781538331293 (6 pack)
Subjects: LCSH: Computer programming–Juvenile literature. | Algorithms–Juvenile literature. | Computer science–Mathematics–Juvenile literature.
Classification: LCC QA76.6 F385 2018 | DDC 005.1–dc23

Manufactured in the United States of America

CPSIA Compliance Information: Batch #CS18PK: For further information contact Rosen Publishing, New York, New York at 1-800-237-9932

CONTENTS

STEP BY STEP

It's Monday morning and you have to get ready for school. First, your alarm goes off. Maybe you hit the snooze button. Then you get out of bed and have breakfast. Next, you brush your teeth and get dressed. Before you get dressed, you check the weather. Is it hot or cold? Is it raining? Once you are dressed, you grab your books and run to the bus stop.

Many of the things we do each day require us to follow step-by-step **procedures**. Before your mother drives to work, she has to unlock the car, fasten her seatbelt, start the engine, and put the car in drive. When your father makes dinner, he probably follows a recipe. Each of these requires you to follow a series of steps to complete a task or solve a problem.

Think of all of the decisions you make when you get ready in the morning. Each decision affects the next step in the process. >

4

ALGORITHMS IN MATH CLASS

You use algorithms every day in math class and probably never realized it. Addition, subtraction, multiplication, and division are examples of simple algorithms. An algorithm is a special set of rules used to do math **calculations** and other problem-solving operations.

THE FATHER OF ALGEBRA

Muhammad ibn Mūsā al-Khwārizmī was born in Persia around AD 780. Al-Khwārizmī was one of the learned men who worked in the House of Wisdom, a scientific research and teaching center. A mathematician and astronomer, al-Khwārizmī created the step-by-step calculations that would become algebra. The word *algorithm* comes from the Latin translation of al-Khwārizmī's name.

When you solve an algebraic equation in math class, you're using an algorithm.

Algebra is one branch of mathematics. With algebra, you can use one step at a time to calculate an unknown value. To solve an algebraic **equation**, it is important to follow all of the steps in the correct order. Skipping a step—or doing step four before step three—will result in a wrong answer. A computer program is a lot like an algebraic equation. Computer programs must follow step-by-step instructions to perform tasks correctly.

SEARCHES AND SPREADSHEETS

Computers have become important tools in our everyday lives. We use computers to shop, watch movies, do our homework, and keep in touch with family and friends. Every task performed by a computer requires a program. And every program requires algorithms to function correctly.

Have you ever used a search engine to locate information? Do your parents use spreadsheets to keep track of household finances? If the answer to either of these questions is yes, then you've used an algorithm. A search engine uses algorithms to rank and sort search results. They appear in order of how **relevant** the result is to your search and how popular that result is. Spreadsheets use algorithms to sort and search data and to perform math calculations.

COMPUTER CONNECTION

A Boolean search is a search that uses the words *and, or,* or *not* between search terms to help narrow your search results.

You've probably had to do an Internet search when doing a report for school. You might not have known that algorithms play a role in making search engines work **efficiently**.

WHAT IS A COMPUTER PROGRAM?

Computers are useless without programs. A program tells a computer how to solve a specific problem. Many of the problems that people use computers to solve are large and complicated. Sometimes, these programs need to be broken down into smaller, simpler steps.

All computer programs have the same basic steps. The first step is the input. Input is the information that we, the users, provide. Input can be the characters you type on a keyboard or the movements you make on a video game controller. In the second step, the computer takes the input and **manipulates** it in some way. This is called a procedure. The final step is the output. Output can be text displayed on a monitor, pages printed from a printer, or the actions of a video game character.

Whether you use the physical keyboard on a laptop or the virtual keyboard on your smartphone or tablet, all computers require input from the user.

INPUT AND OUTPUT FOR VARIOUS KINDS OF PROGRAMS

WORD PROCESSOR

INPUT
Characters typed on keyboard

PROCEDURE
Formats text

OUTPUT
Displays and prints formatted text

VIDEO GAME

INPUT
Keystrokes or joystick movements

PROCEDURE
Calculates how fast and how far to move figures on screen

OUTPUT
Moves a figure on screen

WEB BROWSER

INPUT
HTML (hypertext markup language) code on another computer

PROCEDURE
Converts HTML code into text and graphics

OUTPUT
Displays web pages on screen

RECIPES, PROCEDURES, AND FLOWCHARTS

Computer programs make computers **execute** a series of instructions, step by step. Computer programs follow each step until the end goal of the program is reached. Programs tell computers what steps need to be followed. Algorithms tell the programs how to follow each step.

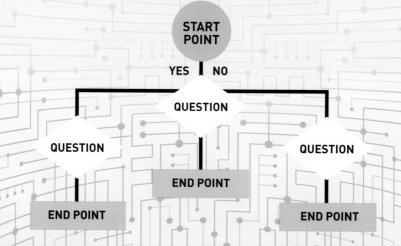

THE PARTS OF A FLOWCHART

While flowcharts might look like just a random collection of shapes, each step makes up a particular part of the flowchart. The starting point is represented by a circle. Each step in the process is represented by a rectangle. Any step that requires a decision to be made, usually a simple "yes" or "no" question, is represented by a diamond. The end point of the process is represented by a rectangle.

Do you like to cook? Following the steps of a recipe is a lot like a computer program following the steps of an algorithm.

Let's use the example of making dinner. An algorithm is like a recipe you would use to prepare a meal. A recipe lists all of the ingredients you need and the steps you need to follow to combine the ingredients in the correct way. The ingredients you use are the input. The meal you will later enjoy is the output. Mixing and cooking the ingredients are the steps that make up the procedure.

An algorithm should be simple and efficient. It should have a clear beginning and an obvious end. There can be as many steps in the middle as are required, and these steps can be repeated many times, if needed. Once an algorithm is written, the computer program will perform the operation the same way, over and over again.

Programmers write out an algorithm before they translate it to a specific **coding language**, such as JavaScript or Python. There are different ways to write out an algorithm. Algorithms can be written as a series of steps in simple text or as a flowchart using shapes and arrows. The first step is always the same; it starts the procedure. The final step always ends the procedure.

COMPUTER CONNECTION

Pseudocode is a special language invented by computer programmers to help them write out algorithms before translating the algorithms into the specific coding language used by the program.

```
(typeOfFID == "REAL"):    value = f
(numOfdot == -1):    tmpFormat = 14 #
lace("czFieldID",str(key)) tempString
lace("czData",str(int(value*pow(10,14
lace + tempString    elif(typeOfFID ==
buffer tempString = tempString.replac
lace + tempString    elif(typeOfFID ==
lace("czDataType","Buffer") tempStrim
or line in searchlines: if "<Name val
ame = searchObj1.group(1) if "</Messa
RicName+"\t"+opaqueV+"\t"+onlyFilena
me = ""    opaqueV = ""    if not os.path.
rt shutil if os.path.exists("Input4RT
es() fo            content:    searchObj
                                or filenam
                                MIre I)
```

Countless programming languages are in use today. But whatever the language, they can all be used to write algorithms.

THE MOST COMMON ALGORITHMS

The two most common kinds of algorithms used in programming are searching algorithms and sorting algorithms. Linear search algorithms are useful when searching for data in relatively short lists. Linear searches start with the first item on the list and check each item in the sequence. Binary searches are better at dealing with large sets of data. A binary search repeatedly cuts a list of data in half until it locates the correct information.

TYPES OF SORTING ALGORITHMS

BUCKET SORT: The data is divided into a number of smaller lists, called "buckets." The data is then sorted and redistributed to the larger list.

MERGE SORT: Compares two already-sorted lists and merges them into a third list.

BUBBLE SORT: An algorithm that sorts a list by comparing two adjacent pieces of data at a time.

QUICK SORT: Divides a list into two smaller lists and then sorts the smaller lists.

Sorting data makes it easier to find when you need it. Think of how easy it is to find a book at your local library because of the Dewey Decimal System.

Computers spend a lot of time sorting massive amounts of data. This is why a lot of work has been done creating different kinds of sorting algorithms. Sorting algorithms take input, in the form of a long list of data, and perform specific operations, such as alphabetizing a list of names. The algorithm then produces output in the form of a sorted list.

CLASSIFICATIONS OF ALGORITHMS

Searching and sorting might be the most common kinds of algorithms, but they're not the only kinds. There are many different classifications, or types, of algorithms used in computer programming. Algorithms can be classified by how they perform, like a recursive algorithm, or how they were designed, like a brute-force algorithm.

A recursive algorithm first solves a small problem. Then it uses that method to solve another version of that problem. A recursive algorithm references itself over and over until the task is completed. These kinds of algorithms often use programming loops—sequences that are carried out several times.

COMPUTER CONNECTION

In computer science, a "stack" is a collection of data. Data can be added, which is called "pushing." The most recent piece of data can also be removed, called "popping."

These crates are a perfect representation of stacks of data. New crates can be added to a stack, and only the most recently added crate can be removed without destroying the entire stack.

A serial algorithm can only do one step of an algorithm at a time. A parallel algorithm takes advantage of computers that have multiple **processors** that can work on multiple steps at the same time. Algorithms that need multiple computers connected with a network are called distributed algorithms.

A brute-force algorithm is sometimes called an exhaustive search algorithm. It tries every possible solution to a problem until it discovers the best one. A divide-and-conquer algorithm takes a problem and repeatedly reduces it to smaller problems. Once small enough, the problems are easy to solve. A greedy algorithm is one that makes what it determines to be the best choice at each step of the process with the hope that it will reach the correct final outcome. Although they may be accurate at a given step, greedy algorithms rarely produce the correct final result.

Algorithms can contain hundreds or thousands of steps. Having multiple computers connected to a network means they can all work on the algorithm together, saving time.

21

MUSIC AND MOVIES

If you regularly share photos, music, or videos on the web, then you probably know what file compression is. File compression takes large files, like your favorite album or movie, and makes them smaller. Smaller files use less **bandwidth**, meaning they can be downloaded or transferred much faster.

There are two kinds of file compression algorithms: lossless compression and lossy compression. As the name implies, lossless compression compresses all of the data contained in a file. Imagine that this string of letters represents a data file: AAABBBBBBCDDDDDDD. A lot of the information is repeated, making the list quite long. The letters can be compressed and written like this: A3B6C1D7. Lossy compression makes files smaller by deleting unnecessary data, like the sounds in a music file that the human ear can't hear.

COMPUTER CONNECTION

Repeatedly using lossy compression on a file removes more and more data from the original. This results in an image or song that is of lower quality than the original.

22

Many people have hundreds of songs stored on their smartphone. Algorithms make it possible to keep files small, meaning they take up less space on a computer or mobile device.

23

RESIZING AND RETOUCHING

It may not seem like it, but algorithms are a key component in graphic design, computer animation, and image manipulation. A lot of factors in graphic design, such as screen sizes and **resolution**, rely on automated mathematical calculations. Colors, fonts, and type styles have all been categorized and indexed. All of this required the use of algorithms.

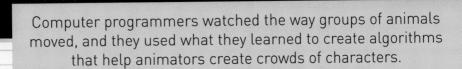

Computer programmers watched the way groups of animals moved, and they used what they learned to create algorithms that help animators create crowds of characters.

Nagle's algorithm is used in computer graphics. It makes **buffering** more efficient. Instead of sending data in multiple small pieces, called packets, this algorithm combines several smaller packets into a single, larger packet, which is then output by the sender. Computer animators use programs that rely on algorithms based on the movement patterns of flocks of birds and herds of animals. These algorithms can be used to make crowds of animated characters that move and behave realistically.

25

KEEPING SECRETS

You've probably heard the word "encryption" before. Encryption is the process of converting ordinary text, called plaintext, into a cipher. The cipher, or ciphertext, can't be understood unless it is decoded, or decrypted. Encryption has been around for thousands of years. Governments and the military have often used it to send and receive important information.

In the digital age, encryption has become more important than ever before. Every time we send our

KEY ENCRYPTION TERMS

BLOCK CIPHER: Algorithms that encrypt chunks, or blocks, of data to create a ciphertext.

CIPHER ALGORITHM: A way to encrypt or decrypt a message.

PUBLIC KEY ENCRYPTION: A way to use a public key to encrypt a message and a private key to decrypt it.

SYMMETRIC ENCRYPTION ALGORITHM: An algorithm in which the encryption key and the decryption key are related to each other. They may even be the same.

To protect it from hackers and other criminals, most important data stored on computers and the Internet is encrypted. Algorithms make it possible to create stronger and safer encryptions.

personal or financial information over the Internet, it could be intercepted by criminals. Websites use algorithms to encrypt sensitive data before it is transferred over the Internet. Companies also use encryption to keep their stored data safe and secure. Of course, hackers can still steal this information if they can find a stronger algorithm to decrypt the encoded information.

A FACE IN THE CROWD

Computer algorithms have been used for some time to identify people based on the unique patterns of their fingerprints. These algorithms are also used by the fingerprint scanners that can be found in some smartphones. Now, although it may seem like something out of a science-fiction movie, algorithms can be used to identify people in photographs.

Facial recognition programs use algorithms to identify "landmarks" on the image of a face. These landmarks include the size, shape, and position of the eyes, nose, cheekbones,

COMPUTER CONNECTION

Biometrics is a way of using facial recognition, fingerprints, retina scans, voice patterns, and other biological data as a means of confirming someone's identity.

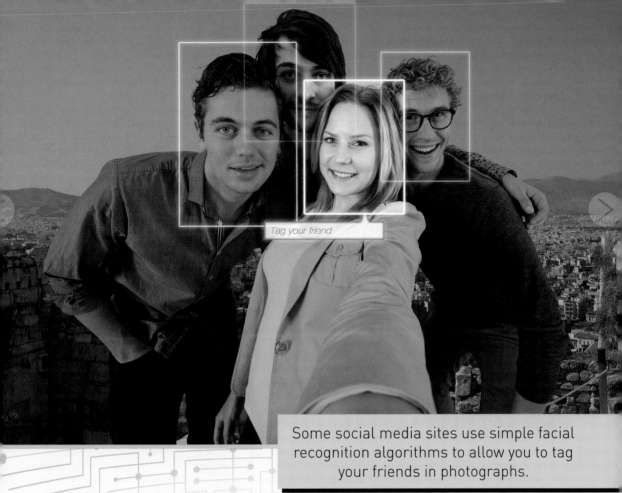

Tag your friend

Some social media sites use simple facial recognition algorithms to allow you to tag your friends in photographs.

chin, and jaw. The facial recognition program then searches an image database for images that may contain similar landmarks. Facial recognition algorithms may not be perfect, but someday, they'll be able to help reduce the amount of time that law enforcement agencies spend trying to identify possible suspects.

WRITING YOUR OWN ALGORITHM

Algorithms play an important role in many aspects of our day-to-day lives. From search engines to file sharing to online shopping, we use algorithms all the time. Now that you've read about algorithms in action, you might want to try to write your own. Choose a task that you do every day and break it down into steps. Write down each step, either as a list or as a flowchart. Run through each step, making sure that the end result of your new algorithm matches the end result that you wanted.

Maybe you think you're ready to try writing algorithms for computer programs. You can take a computer class and learn a programming language, such as Python or JavaScript. Once you get the basics down, writing algorithms should be a breeze.

GLOSSARY

bandwidth: The speed at which data can be transferred.

buffer: To move data into a temporary storage area.

calculate: To find the solution to a problem using math processes.

coding language: A unique language used to write software.

efficient: Capable of producing desired results without wasting materials, time, or energy.

equation: A formal statement of the equality of mathematical expressions.

execute: To carry out or put into effect, such as a plan.

manipulate: To adapt or change something to suit one's need.

procedure: A series of steps followed in a set order.

processor: The key component of a computing device.

relevant: Having significant bearing on the matter at hand.

resolution: The measure of clarity of an image.

INDEX

WEBSITES

Due to the changing nature of Internet links, PowerKids Press has developed an online list of websites related to the subject of this book. This site is updated regularly Please use this link to access the list: www.powerkidslinks.com/eccs/algor